RAMADAN

by Susan L. Douglass
illustrations by Jeni Reeves

On My Own
HOLIDAYS

 Carolrhoda Books, Inc./Minneapolis

To the children who helped with this book: Maryam, Sarah, Karima and Omran — S. D.

To Münevver and Mukaddes — J. R.

The illustrator would like to thank her models: Surria, Hanan, Najeeb,and Bashir Fadel as well as Sharron, Aubrey, and Jade McEmeel and Stuart Reeves. Many thanks to Imam Taha Tawil of the Islamic Cultural and Heritage Center and America's Mother Mosque in Cedar Rapids. His insights and author Susan Douglass's were essential to my understanding of Islam.

Text copyright © 2004 by Susan L. Douglass
Illustrations copyright © 2004 by Jeni Reeves

This book is available in two editions:
Library binding by Carolrhoda Books, Inc., a division of Lerner Publishing Group
Soft cover by First Avenue Editions, an imprint of Lerner Publishing Group
241 First Avenue North
Minneapolis, MN 55401 U.S.A.

Website address: www.lernerbooks.com

Library of Congress Cataloging-in-Publication Data

Douglass, Susan L. (Susan Lynn), 1950–
    Ramadan / by Susan L. Douglass ; illustrations by Jeni Reeves.
       p.   cm. — (On my own holidays)
    Summary: An introduction to Islamic observances during the month of Ramadan and the subsequent festival of Eid-al-Fitr.
    ISBN: 0–87614–932–8 (lib. bdg. : alk. paper)
    1. Ramadan—Juvenile literature. 2. Eid al-Fitr—Juvenile literature. 3. Holidays—Juvenile literature. [1. Ramadan. 2. Eid al-Fitr. 3. Holidays. 4. Islam—Customs and practices.] I. Reeves, Jeni, ill. II. Title. III. On my own holidays
    BP186.4 .D68 2004
    297.3'62—dc21   2002006781

Manufactured in the United States of America
1 2 3 4 5 6 – JR – 09 08 07 06 05 04

Ramadan is an important time of year
for Muslims all over the world.
During Ramadan,
Muslims everywhere fast each day.
Together, they go without food
or drink.
The Ramadan fast lasts
for about four weeks.
It is a way for Muslims everywhere
to honor and obey God.

More than one billion people
around the world are Muslims.
They live in Asia, Africa, Europe,
Australia, and North and South America.
Muslims from many parts of the world
live in the United States and Canada.
The religion that Muslims follow is Islam.
Their name for God is Allah.

Their holy book is called the Quran.

The Quran is written in

the Arabic language.

The Quran tells of many prophets.

The prophets were teachers sent by Allah

to show people how to live a good life.

Muslims believe that Muhammad was

the last prophet.

Muslims believe that Allah gave Muhammad
the Quran long ago.
It is said that the first words of the Quran
came to Muhammad one night
during the time of Ramadan.
The Quran tells Muslims to fast
during Ramadan each year.
During this month, Muslims go without
food or drink all day.
They begin to fast each day at dawn.
After the sun sets,
they eat and drink once again.
Ramadan is a time when Muslims
all over the world honor Allah together.

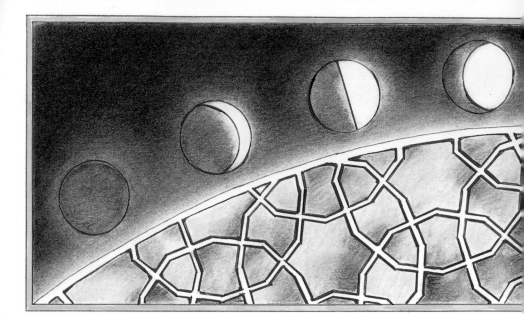

The Month of Ramadan

To know the day of the month,

most people look at a calendar.

Long ago, people counted the months

by the changing shape of the moon.

Every month, the moon seems to disappear.

Then it is called a new moon.

The next day, the new moon appears

like a thin slice of apple.

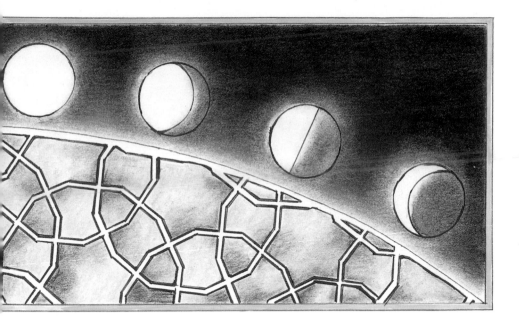

The moon grows as the days pass.

In the middle of the month,

the moon shines

full and round.

Then it gets smaller and smaller,

until it disappears again.

The changes a moon goes through is

called a cycle.

Muslims use the moon's cycle
for their religious calendar.
Twelve moon cycles make up
the Islamic year.
Ramadan is the ninth month.
The Ramadan fast begins when
the new moon of Ramadan appears.
Ramadan comes in different seasons.
Over many years, Ramadan moves
through summer, fall, winter, and spring.
Muslims use computers to know
when Ramadan is near.
Muslims everywhere wait
for the ninth new moon.
They watch for it in high places
and open spaces.

When people in one place see
the new moon, news travels fast.
Muslim leaders announce it
on radio and TV.
People call family members.
It's Ramadan tomorrow!

In one Muslim country,
children carry lanterns
through the streets.
They sing a song to welcome Ramadan.
An important time of honoring Allah
has begun.

The Day Begins

Each day of Ramadan,

Muslims wake up very early.

In many countries, drummers go through

the streets in the early morning.

Boom, ba-boom! Boom, ba-ba-boom!

They wake people

while it is still dark outside.

The drummer calls out,

"Wake up from sleep, All!

God is Eternal!"

Sleepy grown-ups and children

slide out of bed.

Before the sun rises,
everyone eats a meal called suhoor.
Suhoor gives Muslims energy
to get through the long day of fasting.
To make sure the sleepyheads eat,
parents let children choose
their favorite foods.
In the United States, families may have
an American breakfast.

After the meal,

the family prays before sunrise.

This is the first prayer of the day.

Muslims pray at five different times

during each day.

Muslim families pray together

whenever they can.

A Time of Fasting

Not everyone has to fast during Ramadan.

Anyone who is sick or old

does not have to fast.

Women who are expecting a baby

do not have to fast.

Many children fast for part of Ramadan.

But children do not have to fast.

Some children fast
from the suhoor meal
until lunchtime.
Others fast for only a few days
of the month.
For young Muslims,
the important thing is to try.

Trying to be a good person all day is
another part of fasting during Ramadan.
Fasting does not just mean
going without food or drink.
For Muslims, fasting also means
trying not to be angry or unkind.
People try to be patient with each other
when they are fasting.
They forgive each other when a person
does something wrong.

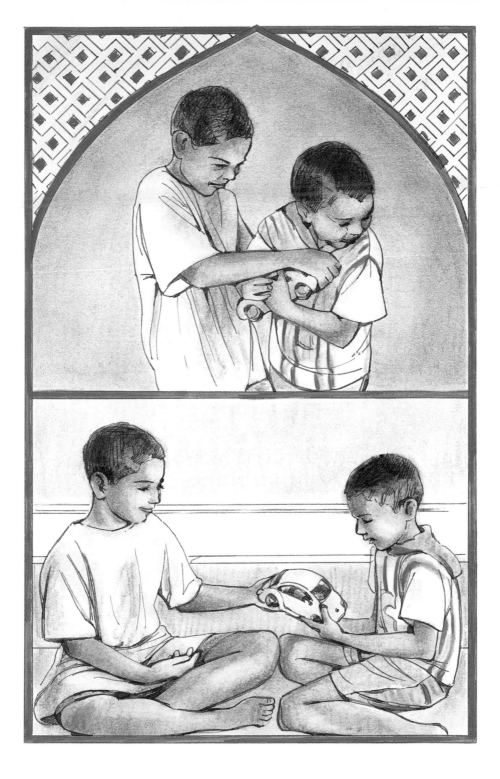

Fasting can make it hard
for Muslims to stay awake
and do regular work.
Sometimes, fasting students
feel sleepy at school.
In the United States,
some schools have a room
where fasting students can rest.

Students go to the room instead of going
to the cafeteria for lunch.
They also go to the room at noon
to pray the second daily prayer.
After school or work,
many Muslims take a short nap.
They wake up in time for the third prayer
in midafternoon.

Countdown to Sundown

The kitchen is a busy place near sundown.

Cooking pots are steaming.

Food simmers with the smell of spices.

Guests often come to share

the evening meal.

They bring a favorite dish to share.

Before sundown,

the table is set and the food is covered.

The covered dishes look like

wrapped gifts at a party.

The clock ticks on the wall.
Someone checks his watch.
Another person checks a chart
on the wall.
The chart tells what time sunset
will come each day.
For everyone, the clock seems to tick
more slowly at this part of the day.

In Muslim cities and villages,
the call to prayer sounds at sunset.
The call comes from tall towers
and loudspeakers.
It comes from radio and television.
"Allahu Akbar!"
This call means "God is Great!"
The words echo through the neighborhoods.
The fast has ended for the day.

Muslims break their fast by eating
just a little food at first.
A few juicy dates and cool water
is enough.
This is how their prophet Muhammad
broke his fast long ago.
After breaking the fast,
Muslims pray the short sunset prayer.
This is the fourth prayer of the day.

After the sunset prayer, Muslims enjoy
the main Ramadan meal.
This meal is called iftar.
Soup, salad, meat stew, rice, noodles,
bread, and sweet desserts with tea
make iftar meals.
Each country has its own special
iftar dishes.
Many families have
their own recipes, too.

Some Muslims enjoy iftar at their
place of worship.
This place is called
a mosque or a masjid.
Others give money or food
for the meal served there.
Anyone who comes to the masjid will be
given the iftar meal.
Sharing food with people in need
is another important part of Ramadan.

After iftar, families join together
at the masjid for special prayers.
First, they gather for the evening prayer.
It is the fifth prayer of the day.
Rows and rows of people
fill the large space.
Men's and boys' rows are in front.
Women, girls, and small children
stand in back.
Everyone stands shoulder to shoulder,
bowing and kneeling.
Older boys and girls join their parents
in the masjid during all the prayers.
Younger children in classrooms draw
pictures, learn songs, and play games.
At the end of Ramadan,
the children often put on plays.

During special Ramadan prayers,
Muslims hear the whole Quran
read aloud.
The man who reads is called a qari.
Each night, the qari reads a part
of the Quran with a beautiful voice.
Hundreds of voices reply, "Amen."

One special night near the end
of Ramadan is called the Night of Power.
On the Night of Power, Muslim families
stay at the masjid all night.
They remember how the Quran
first came to Muhammad
on that same night long ago.
They pray until the first morning light.

Ramadan is Over!

After 29 or 30 days of fasting,
Ramadan comes to an end.
Once again, Muslims around the world
wait for the new moon to appear.
The next day will be a great celebration
called Eid al-Fitr.
It means the "Feast of Breaking the Fast."
Eid al-Fitr lasts three days.
It is a time for Muslims to celebrate
the challenges they met together
during Ramadan.

Muslim families everywhere get ready
for Eid al-Fitr.
Each family must give
food or money
to people in need.

Families also clean and decorate their homes.

They prepare sweet treats.

They buy gifts for the children.

Many children get new clothes and shoes
at the end of Ramadan.

Eid al-Fitr Is Here!

Some countries are home to many Muslims.

In these Muslim countries,

the streets are decorated for Eid al-Fitr.

People in towns and cities put up lights,

banners, and balloons.

When the weather is nice,

Eid al-Fitr celebrations are held outdoors.

In American cities,
Eid al-Fitr celebrations take place
in parks or large indoor spaces.
Smaller Muslim communities
celebrate at the masjid.
Some families travel to large cities
for the celebration.

After sunrise on Eid al-Fitr,
Muslims all over the world get ready.
Everyone puts on their best clothes.
They go to the place of celebration
for an Eid prayer.
The Eid prayer is the same everywhere.

Thousands of people line up
in straight rows to pray.
They stand, bow, and kneel all together
like waves rolling onto a beach.
Then they sit and listen
to the prayer leader's speech.

After the prayer, the people rise
and greet each other.
They all say, "Eid mubarak!"
It is a greeting of blessings
and good wishes.
Grown-ups give money and candy
to children.
There are games and picnics.
Many outdoor celebrations have rides.
Some have Ferris wheels and carousels.
Others have ponies or elephants to ride.
The celebration goes on until evening.
For the next two or three days, families
visit each other and share delicious treats.

Muslim children enjoy
the celebration.
They are proud of the fasting they did
during Ramadan.
Next year, Muslims everywhere will fast
for Allah once again.

An Iftar Recipe
Cucumber-Mint Yogurt Dip

Ingredients

1 medium cucumber

2 cups plain yogurt

2 tablespoons olive oil (or a little more to taste)

1 teaspoon dried crushed mint or 1 tablespoon fresh
chopped mint

salt to taste

1 package pita bread

Directions

1. Peel cucumber. Grate by hand into a bowl.

2. Drain off extra cucumber juice.

3. Add yogurt, olive oil, mint, and salt. Stir until
well mixed.

4. Taste. Add more salt and olive oil if needed.

5. Toast pita bread and cut or tear into pieces.

6. Dip bread in yogurt dip. Enjoy!

New Words

Allah (ahl-LAHH): the name for God in the Arabic language

Eid al-Fitr (EED ahl-FIHTR): Feast of Breaking the Fast, a celebration at the end of Ramadan

Eid mubarak! (EED moo-BAHR-ahk): a greeting for the Eid al-Fitr celebration

Iftar (ihf-TAHR): the meal in Ramadan that breaks the fast

Islam (ihss-LAM): a religion of belief in one God, in prophets such as Abraham, Moses, Jesus, and Muhammad, and their holy books

masjid (MASS-jihd): the traditional Arabic term for a mosque

mosque (MAHSK): a building where Muslims pray

Muslims (MUHSS-lihms): people who follow Islam

qari (KAHR-ee): reader, a person who recites the Quran in a beautiful voice

Quran (koor-AHN): the holy book of Islam

Ramadan (rah-mah-DAHN): month of fasting for Muslims. It is the ninth month of the Islamic calendar.

suhoor (sah-HOOR): the early breakfast Muslims eat before fasting